The Student Millionaire

A guide for Young Adults to find *THEIR* path to their *FIRST* Million Dollars!

By
Rich Patenaude

www.TheStudentMillionaire.com

Table of Contents

Dedication

This book is dedicated to my wonderful family: Blythe, my wife, the family's sparkler of ideas; Chris, my son and Mr. Personality, who will no doubt be Mr. President someday; and my lovely daughter, Angela, whose natural beauty is outshone only by her heart of gold.

Acknowledgements

This leg of my journey began with a trip from Washington, D.C. to Tampa, Florida to spend a day with professional speaking coach Alfonso Castaneira. That trip was the starting point of sharing my passion with young adults on how to become a millionaire. That passion turned into articles, which in turn led me to attend Brendon Burchard's Experts Academy, which in turn led me to write this book. All this occurred in the space of 12 months.

Of equal importance is the roll of the dice I took by attending the CEO Space International forum in March 2011. CEO Space International is the gift that keeps on giving, the investment that keeps on yielding results, benefits and dividends for years to come. Every contact on this page for which I am enormously grateful is the result of my attending that incredible forum. I am particularly indebted to Berny Dohrmann, the organization's Founder, Chairman and CEO, for his supernatural efforts on behalf of the organization and its members. I have personally benefitted from Berny's coaching and good counsel on at least a half dozen occasions.

Kathie Callahan-Brady. is an incredibly talented lady who has been both a friend and a mentor throughout this process. Her guidance, wisdom and occasional tough love have served me well as a guiding light and a constant in this segment of my adventure. As the one who coined my title of Wealth Coach to Young Adults, Kathie will surely recognize her influence and imprint throughout this project.

There are many others I could mention here: supporters, investors, coaches, editors, writers, proofreaders, and many good friends. Please know that you have earned my deepest gratitude for the role you have played in my success.

RP

Foreword

Welcome to The Student Millionaire community. You have taken the brave and courageous step to explore just how abundance can be brought about in your life.

Congratulations on being willing to step outside of the box and take a different path than the one most people do. As a young adult reading this book, you are taking the first step on an exciting journey that will change your life and the life of the people around you forever.

The principles you will be taught in this book are not new. Some have been around for centuries or even longer. Others have been formally introduced into mainstream thinking only in the last hundred years or so.

But taken together, these principles provide you with a guide, a blueprint if you will, that maps out what you need to do to create and attract your first million dollars. That's right; I said your FIRST million dollars. Not your ONLY million dollars. I say this because once you have done the work and achieved your first million, you will already have the tools in place to create your second million, and then your third million, and so on, if you choose to do so.

In this book you'll discover that the most critical thing you can do to bring yourself to this point is simply to decide today, once and for all, that you WILL be a millionaire and do whatever it takes (legally) to get yourself there. This simple decision is a most profound moment in your life that will set everything else in motion that you need to accomplish and achieve your goal. I cannot overstate this point. This is absolutely critical and central to your success. Without your committed and firm decision to become a Millionaire, you are not likely to ever become one. Period. More on this later.

The reason I make this point so strongly is because 80% of what is needed to attract abundance, or anything else in your life, happens inside of you. It does not depend on what happens outside of you – people, events and circumstances. I know, at first glance, this doesn't seem to make much sense and is hard to believe. It is counterintuitive, as in, it's not likely something that you would expect to normally be the case. This is really hard for most people to understand and accept. But trust me. I will make this clearer and explain it in detail as you make your way through the book.

As you have probably gathered from reading this Foreword, being a Millionaire requires you to think differently from the way you are used to. This is called the Millionaire Mindset: how you view, filter, approach and process your information. Through the ages, the wise and learned men of their times invariably taught that as a whole your thoughts pretty much determine and control your life. That's a pretty powerful statement, especially if you have never thought of it this way before. You may not have control over your circumstances. But you do have control over your thoughts, which in turn control your circumstances. And just knowing this provides you with an incredibly powerful tool to shape your life the way you want it to be, the way you choose it to be.

Again, welcome to The Student Millionaire community. I am so excited for you and the journey you have decided to take. Your life will never again be the same. From this point on, your life will start to take the shape YOU give it. This will begin fairly quickly. And as it does, know that YOU are now writing your own script. YOU are in charge. YOU are in control. YOU are now master of your own life! So let's get on with it.

Here's to your success!

Rich Patenaude

P.S. If you wish to be part of our Student Millionaire community, please visit us at **www.TheStudentMillionaire.com** and sign up. We'd love to have you be a member of our Millionaire Club.

Chapter One – The Decision

Once you make a decision, the universe conspires to make it happen.

Ralph Waldo Emerson

Outside of getting married and having children, your decision to be a millionaire, no matter what, is the most pivotal decision you will ever make in your life. Period. It affects everything. Being a millionaire affects where you live. It affects what you do with your time. It affects who you choose to associate with in your life. It affects what you can do to help others. It gives you the freedom to pursue your interests and be the person you are meant to be. In short, being a millionaire allows you to live the way you are meant to live, and to live the life you were born to live.

So decide today, right now, that you will be a millionaire no matter what, no matter what obstacles may come your way, no matter what self-doubts you may have. As of today, you are now totally and completely focused on manifesting your first million dollars as your top priority. It will constantly be in the forefront of your mind and in your daily thoughts. You will read this book in its entirety, and reread it several times until the principles in it become second nature to you. You will follow through on the prescribed action steps to be taken. You will push through any negative thoughts that bubble up about being able to do this, about being worthy to do this, about whether this can be done, about whether this is possible for you. Because it is.

Being a millionaire is not only possible for you, it's inevitable. By following these principles, it's possible for anyone and everyone to be a millionaire. But for the moment, let's just take care of you.

Here you are at a crossroad in your life. You have chosen to pick up and read this book, maybe out of curiosity, maybe just to see what the fuss is all about. Maybe you want to read a few chapters first before you decide to be a millionaire. You may not be sure this is for you. Really? If someone came up to you and offered you a million dollars in cash, no strings attached, would you think twice about it? Or would you take it, say "thank you," and get on with your life?

It's time. It's your time. So take a deep breath. There is no better time for you to decide to be a millionaire than now, than today. So get on with it. Give yourself the gift of wealth. If you have already done so, I congratulate you for having the courage to take this step to move your life forward in this direction. You are on your way to an extraordinary life of your choosing and design.

If you have not already done so, then do so now, and start your new life today, this very moment. The decision will change your life forever.

OK, are we good? You've made your decision to be a millionaire? Great. Remember, there's no turning back. There's only moving forward. Let your journey begin.

Like bungee jumping off a cliff for the first time, the experience can be a little scary. Probably a lot scary. But the more you do it, the easier it gets, so they say. So what scares you the most about being a millionaire? Is it that you can't imagine yourself doing it, accomplishing it, achieving it? Is it because the first question that comes to mind is "How on earth can I possibly do something like that?!" "What will people think of me?" Or at some level and for some reason, do you not feel worthy to be a millionaire? Don't worry, people will think you're pretty cool.

Whatever your greatest fear, whatever your burning issue is when it comes to money, making money, having a lot of money and being a millionaire, you can deal with it, you can work your way through it. It's just one more dragon you have to slay along the way to your castle. So start slaying.

Take a few minutes with a pad of paper and pen and some quiet time. Find a quiet place where you will not be disturbed for a few minutes. Turn off your cell phone, your computer and anything else that might disrupt your concentration. Once you're comfortable, at the top of the page, write $1,000,000 large enough so it stares you in the face. Then underneath it, write "What issues do I have about earning, attracting into my life, and creating for myself, this amount of money?"

Take a deep breath, close your eyes, and ponder those questions. Give yourself a few minutes and see what bubbles up for you. Then start writing down everything that comes up for you – whatever it is. This process is called stream of consciousness. It allows you to tap your innermost thoughts and feelings about any subject. What comes up is what comes up. What is revealed is what is revealed. It is what it is. Don't question it. Don't qualify it. Don't worry about the wording. Just write it out. And let it come out. And keep writing until you have nothing left to write.

You'll probably be amazed at what bubbles up. Remember, you're looking for worthiness issues, confidence issues, money issues, and the like – anything that for you might represent a barrier or obstacle in your quest for your first million dollars. Don't be upset or ashamed about anything that comes up. Don't be alarmed either. It's all good. The most important thing for you is to let it come up so you can put your finger on what lurks beneath your surface, what might prevent you from achieving your goal, and slay that dragon. Chances are you never even knew it was there.

This is how you find out what scripts are running inside you on these issues. We'll discuss this in more detail later in the book. Don't worry about them for now. Just write it down and set whatever comes up aside in a safe place. We'll come back to it later. I do invite you to read it, however, so you can have an idea of what you're dealing with. But don't overreact or over-analyze it at this point. Your main job is only to get this stuff out, your dragons, if you will, that lurk inside of you, on paper so that you can analyze, dissect and slay these dragons as we move you on your way to your million-dollar goal.

If nothing comes up right away, don't worry about it. It will. Almost everyone has issues about money in one way or another. Just set your pad of paper aside and schedule another session. Make sure your environment is conducive for you to access your thoughts and feelings within. Quiet. No distractions. Cell phone and everything else turned off. Nothing to distract or disturb you. Then give it another try.

If you happen to be in the very small minority of individuals that has no negative issues when it comes to being a millionaire, then count your blessings. You have no dragons to slay and you can move on with your journey to become a millionaire. You are well on your way. But you are rare indeed.

Either way, you are now ready to move on into this new world of thinking like a millionaire. This new way of thinking is different from what you are used to. It requires focus, intent, dedication, commitment and determination. From this point on, YOU control your thoughts with absolute clarity of purpose. You are no longer easily swayed by the people and circumstances that surround you. You no longer take the unfounded opinions of others as Gospel truth. You think for yourself. Your opinions are based on facts. Everything is filtered through you. YOU orchestrate your life. Your life is not orchestrated for you.

All of this is now possible because you have made the pivotal, critical and unequivocal decision to be a millionaire. You have chosen a new path for yourself. You now have the clear and definite goal to manifest into your life your first million dollars. You have never done this before. This kind of thinking is new to you. You are stepping out into unchartered territory. Not quite sure of yourself as you begin, you develop the courage to keep moving forward in this direction. Unsure about your abilities to accomplish this goal, you begin to trust yourself enough, more and more each day, to continue steadily moving yourself forward toward your goal. Each and every day, you become increasingly confident that you can do this, that this million-dollar goal you have chosen for yourself really is within the realm of possibility for you.

Granted, this is a huge and exciting leap forward fraught with fear and trepidation. Maybe bungee-cord jumping would be easier. Nevertheless, your millionaire journey has begun. There is no turning back. Nor would you want to. Before moving on to the next chapter, take a few minutes to contemplate how different your life would be with a million dollars in the bank. How would your day be different? What would you do with your time? What would be the first thing you would buy for yourself? Who comes to mind when you think about helping someone?

These thoughts give you a sampling of the differences between your current life you are leaving behind, and the one you have chosen to create. Let these new thoughts be part of your motivation as you make your way through this book. Let these new thoughts help you slay your dragons of negative thinking as they come up throughout this process. Let these thoughts help you see the life you can have, if you only believe in yourself enough to give this process a chance.

For what it's worth, you have already done more in this first chapter than most people do in a lifetime, in terms of choosing a definite, life-changing goal and taking the steps to achieve it. I commend you. Don't sell yourself short. This is no small thing. As you will see in the chapters ahead, by making this decision to be a millionaire, you have set the most remarkable wheels in motion that will get you to where you want to go. You have no idea of the powerful forces you have now unleashed.

You are not alone in this journey. People who can help you, that you would never have met otherwise, will now begin to cross your path. Things that would never have happened before will start happening, seemingly like magic, to help you. As all of this unfolds before you, remember to always have a grateful heart. An attitude of gratitude will forever grease the skids of your success.

Action Item:

1. In a quiet place with no distractions (cell phone off, computer off, etc.), take a pad of paper and a pen/pencil and write the amount of $1,000,000 at the top, big enough to make an impression, but leave space below it to write.

2. Underneath that number, write the question: "What issues do I have about earning, attracting into my life, creating for myself, this amount of money?"

3. Take a deep breath, close your eyes for a few minutes and ponder the question.

4. After a few minutes, open your eyes and start writing. Keep writing until there is no more to write and you've emptied everything that was inside of you related to this issue.

5. Review what you've written and set it aside in a safe place. We'll come back to it later.

Chapter Two – The Purpose

True happiness…is not attained through self-gratification but through fidelity to a worthy purpose.

Helen Keller

This Chapter is really about *Your* Purpose and the reason you have chosen to become a millionaire. The reason is for you to be free to become the person you are meant to be, to live the life you are meant to live, and make the unique contribution to the world that only you can make.

Now that you have made the decision to be a millionaire, let's ask the question "Why?" Why do this? Why focus your time, talents, and energy on becoming a millionaire instead of just getting a job? Surely the money from being a millionaire would be nice. Having a million dollars in the bank would certainly eliminate the worry about making ends meet and buying the things you need and want.

Is there more to life and having money than just buying stuff? Is there more to you than just a desire to make and spend money? You know there is. Everyone senses, deep inside, that there is much more to them than they have been able to show the world so far. At some level, everyone knows that they are unique, that they are special. Most people simply haven't been given the opportunity or shown the way to express their uniqueness. It is time you do so, and understand the reason why you should do so.

Ever ask yourself "Why am I here?" Or "What am I supposed to do while I'm here?" Most people never take the time to actually think about these questions. People are usually so bogged down with day-to-day living that they just don't have, or take, the time to think about who they really are and what their purpose might be in this life. They just go about their lives and fill them up with the best things they can, or know how to do at the time – go to school, get a job, raise a family, and so on. These activities which they see everybody else around them doing become, by default, their purpose in life. It's not that you don't get satisfaction from these things. It's just that, somehow, you have a nagging feeling that there is more to life. You can be more. You can do more.

And you're right. You can do more and be more. And it all starts with realizing who you really are. Take a moment to think about this: You could search the entire world of six billion people or so and never, ever, find an exact duplicate of you. One just doesn't exist. They broke the mold when you were born. There never was and never will be another you. You're it. You are one of a kind. There is no one else with your unique set of gifts, talents, interests, and personality. This unique set of attributes, coupled with your unique set of circumstances and life events, help make you who and what you are.

I say 'help' make you who and what you are because there's even more to you than all of this. That individual that is you has the capacity to take these elements and mold them into something that is, again, truly unique. By choosing what you think about and what you focus on, you give shape to the you that you want to become. We'll go over this in more detail in the next chapter. The possible combination of these elements is limited only by your imagination. And what comes out at the other end is always uniquely you.

Let's have a little fun. Get the pad of paper that you used in the first chapter to discover how you feel about money. Flip to a new page. We're going to start discovering who you really are.

At the top of the page, write down these three questions:

1. What makes me happy?
2. What interests me the most?
3. What special gifts, talents, and abilities do I have?

Now take a few minutes with *each* one of these questions individually and write down what comes to mind. Like before, don't question it. Don't qualify it. Don't limit it. Don't judge it. And don't be alarmed by anything that comes up. Just write it down.

Take the time to do this with each of the three questions. Think about the times in your life when you were the happiest. What were the special circumstances or events that made you happy? Who was involved? What was special about them that made you happy? Was it something you were doing alone or with others? Can you put your finger on what it was specifically about these times that made you happy?

Now let's look at the things that interest you the most. Besides being happy, what do you like to do the most with your time? Do you like sports or music? Do you like spending time with your friends or playing video games? How do you spend your free time? How would you choose to spend your time if money weren't a limitation? If you could spend your time doing anything you wanted to do, what would that be?

Now take a look at the special gifts, talents and abilities you have. Are you good with people? Do you have lots of friends? Or are you the quiet type who prefers to spend time alone and think about things? What are you good at? Are you particularly good as an athlete or musician? Do you ever dream about doing something that just seems out of reach? If you could learn to do something new, what would that be? Are you mechanical? Do you like tinkering with your hands?

Maybe you don't think you have any special skills. You're wrong. Everyone can do something. Maybe you're great at cooking and cleaning house. Maybe you do a great job at mowing lawns. Maybe you do a great job volunteering someplace where people really need your help. And that something, as simple as it might seem to you at the moment, can lead to something else. Do not discount anything you do. Every talent, every gift, as simple as it might seem to you, is in some way valuable to someone.

Again, this exercise will be very revealing to you. Please give it the time it deserves. It will help you pinpoint what brings you joy in your life, where you like to spend your time and what you enjoy doing with that time.

Once you have done this exercise, take the time to look it over. Did anything come up that surprises you? This snapshot of what makes you happy, what interests you, and what you're good at doing is not set in stone. The more you think about these things, the more things will come up that you may have overlooked. When they do, take the time to jot them down. It's just another piece of the puzzle that will help you get a clearer picture of yourself.

Remember, at the beginning of this chapter we said the reason for being a millionaire is to be free to be the person you are meant to be and to make your unique contribution to the world. By answering the three questions above, you are beginning to take stock of what makes you *you*. You are beginning to appreciate what makes you unique and special. Make time for this. It is time very well spent.

By this process, you are also beginning to identify what avenues you might take on your path to becoming a millionaire based on your gifts, talents and interests. And you are also beginning to identify what your unique contribution to the world might be once you are financially free to make it. It's a process. Let it unfold. Not all the answers to your questions will be made available to you today. Keep your thoughts on your million-dollar goal and stay alert to the thoughts, people and events that come your way that might help you get there. Be sure to continually and automatically reject any negative thoughts, or thoughts of limitation or lack, that might discourage you from pursuing your goal. Stay on track and you'll get there. I promise.

As you make your way through this book, your purpose and the path to your million-dollar goal will become clearer. You will better understand the power of your thoughts, and how your thoughts attract things to you. You will also better understand how powerful a tool you have in your intuition, and how to use it to guide you along your path. And as you learn these things, you will grow in confidence in the knowledge of knowing what to do and how to trust yourself. Trust the process and have faith in yourself. I have faith in you and every confidence that you can do this.

Now imagine you have identified your unique path to making your first million dollars, you have started thinking about a plan, and you have taken the first steps on that path toward your million-dollar goal. Congratulations! You are on your way. You may not know exactly how you will get there. But by making the decision to be a millionaire, examining your special set of gifts and talents, and taking whatever steps in this direction that you can today, you have set the wheels in motion to get yourself there. The key is remaining steadfast in your goal, being alert to what comes up in thoughts and actions, staying positive at all times, and listening to your intuition. More on this later.

Now imagine for a moment that you have arrived – you have achieved your goal of bringing about and making your first million dollars. For the first time in your life, you are completely and financially free to do whatever you want with your time. In the process, you have discovered your special gifts and talents that you used to make your first million dollars. You now have the skills needed to make your second million dollars, and so on.

You now are in the position to start making your unique contribution to the world. What will it be? You can support a cause. You can support a charity. You can start your own charity, if the one you are looking for doesn't exist. You now have the power and opportunity in your life to do good, to bless the lives of others, to help make this world a better place.

This is the reason you became a millionaire: to be the person you were meant to be, to live the life you were born to live, and to make the unique contribution to the world that only you can make. You can take care of yourself, your family and the ones you love. But more than that, you may now be a blessing in the lives of people who may never know your name. You are now that angel who shows up at just the right time and provides that special blessing in the lives of others. You have found, and are now living, your true purpose.

Action Item:

1. Again, in a quiet place with no distractions (cell phone off, computer off, etc.), take out your pad of paper and a pen/pencil and answer the three questions stated below:

   1. What makes me happy?
   2. What interests me the most?
   3. What special gifts, talents, and abilities do I have?

2. Take one question at a time and let your thoughts flow freely.

3. Write down any and all thoughts that come to you. Don't qualify your answers or hold yourself back. Just write what you think about.

4. Be generous to yourself. Give yourself the time needed to do this for each question.

5. When you have finished, review what you've written. You are now starting to get a better idea of what makes you tick. This is not set in stone. The more you take the time to think about these things, the more ideas will come up for you. Take note of them and continue to write them down, as much as possible, as you move through the book.

Chapter Three - The Goal

The establishment of a
clear…goal in life is the starting
point of all success.

Brian Tracy

From this moment forward, your overriding, pivotal, central goal in life is to create your first million dollars.

This is now your #1 goal until the day you achieve it. You may have other educational, professional, and personal goals along the way, but your million-dollar goal is now front and center in your mind until you achieve it. This is the reason you are reading this book. This is what will make everything else in your life fall into place. It's that simple.

Why a million-dollar goal? Why not ten million? Why not start out smaller, say with $10,000 and work your way up?

The million-dollar goal is not set in stone. You can change it anytime you want. I am choosing to give you the million-dollar goal because a million dollars is a definite game-changer in most people's lives. Just imagining being a millionaire is a huge stretch for most people, as it probably is for you. Just the thought of making, earning, and having a million dollars stretches your imagination far beyond the boundaries you have previously set for yourself. And in this day and age, a million-dollar goal is especially attainable.

So go ahead, accept it. Start thinking of yourself as a millionaire. You *are* a *millionaire*. How does it feel? Start enjoying the feeling that comes with being a millionaire. This is all part of the process, as you will see in the next few chapters. Hold that feeling. Cultivate that feeling. Make that feeling a part of you and it will become you. And you will become it – a millionaire.

One of the main things that happens when you start thinking this way is focus. That's what a goal does. It focuses your thoughts. Ask anyone who has ever achieved anything and you'll discover that they absolutely had a goal. Whether large or small, all accomplishments and achievements, without exception, started with a goal. A goal gives your thoughts direction. And these thoughts, in turn, lead you to take the actions needed to achieve your goal. Your goal brings clarity and purpose to your thoughts. And this clarity and purpose, in turn, drives your actions that make your goal a reality.

Your thoughts, which are usually scattered among a million different things, begin to be brought together as you start focusing on your goal. Rather than let your thoughts control you, you now begin to control your thoughts. This is huge. It seems simple enough. But most people fail to realize just how important a role controlling your thoughts plays in how your life unfolds. Your thoughts pretty much determine your life and what kind of reality you create for yourself. If this concept is entirely new to you, it may take some adjusting and getting used to. But know this: Your thoughts determine your life. Control your thoughts, and you control your life. And your goal helps you do just that. Give yourself the gift of this new destination in life.

Another thing that your million-dollar goal does for you is that it galvanizes your thoughts and energies. Your million-dollar goal stimulates, even shocks, you into a new state of mind. That jolt serves to kick you out of your usual stream of humdrum thought and energizes you to new possibilities. This can be unsettling, even frightening, for many. But you absolutely have to fight those negative feelings and thoughts, if and when they come up. Your goal busts you out of your old way of doing things. Your goal now puts you on a new path, one that will change your life and the life of the people around you forever.

Your million-dollar goal not only stretches your imagination and your thoughts, it also stretches you. Your goal pushes you to reach far beyond what you thought you were capable of doing. Later on, we'll talk about the negative and limiting thoughts and beliefs that may come up as you courageously put yourself on this path. You will wonder if this is really possible. You'll ask yourself if you're just kidding yourself. "Who do you think you are to think you can be a millionaire?" and so on.

You have just as much right to be a millionaire as anyone else. You not only have the right, but you are definitely smart enough to do this. You have all the necessary gifts, talents and abilities to get this done. If you can think, you can be a millionaire. Your thoughts are an extraordinarily powerful tool in this process. And your million-dollar goal organizes, focuses and energizes your thoughts to show you the way to get there – *your* unique way to get there.

How will you know that you are doing the right things, that you're moving in the right direction? Your intuition will guide you through all the things that come up. Your intuition is an incredible tool that will tell you whether or not you're on the right path. It will tell you whether or not the things you are doing are the right ones for you. Your intuition will guide you as to who you should talk to, what you should look into, where to go for the information and the resources you need. This is what I mean when I tell you to rely on yourself. You may not have all the answers to the questions you have about reaching your goal, but your intuition does. Rely on it. Your intuition will rarely, if ever, fail you. It will be there when you need it to be. It will guide you when you need guidance. Make your intuition your best friend ever.

Another critically important role that having a goal plays in your life is that it keeps you and your life from drifting and being filled by whatever comes up. It's *your* life. Your life should be filled by the things you choose to fill it with. Your life should not be filled by the random things that others choose for you or that just come your way. If you interview 100 people and ask them why they are doing what they are doing, 98 people will likely answer that they don't know. Everyone else is going to school, working, having children. It's what people do. The obvious thing missing here is the goal. Ask them what exactly they want to accomplish in life, what is their main purpose in life, and only 2 out of 100 are able to answer you with a clear and definite goal. By taking on this million-dollar goal, you are joining that very small elite group of individuals who have a definite goal.

Your million-dollar goal gives you definiteness of purpose. In addition to keeping you from drifting in life and allowing your life to be filled up with whatever comes your way, to be filled with whatever things serendipity chooses for you, definiteness of purpose keeps you on track for your goal in times of adjustment. Many people view temporary failure in one thing as the end-all be-all of their goal. They interpret a temporary setback as a permanent defeat. If one thing doesn't work exactly as they had planned, they just give up. A temporary defeat must mean that their goal just wasn't meant to be.

On the contrary, a temporary defeat is nothing more than an adjustment, time to rethink and retool your plan. A temporary defeat is nothing more than the universe telling you that you need to take a step back and assess what is and isn't working. What is your intuition telling you? What can be done differently? If Thomas Edison had been discouraged every time he failed at inventing the light bulb, where would we be today? The inventor famously said that he did not fail thousands of times in his attempt to come up with the light bulb; he simply discovered thousands of ways the light bulb did not work. Here is a man who had definiteness of purpose. He did not let temporary defeat stop him from pursuing his goal. And wasn't that a good thing for us?

This same principle of definiteness of purpose applies for you in all things. If you pursue each and every goal with the same relentlessness Thomas Edison pursued the development of the light bulb, nothing in the world can prevent you from achieving anything – even creating your first million dollars. You can design your life to be exactly what you want it to be. You can have your million dollars. You can have the home you want, the car you want, to live where you want to live, to do with your time the things you want to do. In other words, you can have your custom-made life exactly as you designed it to be, exactly as you intended it to be. Your life simply becomes the result of your unwavering definiteness of purpose.

Yes, there will be bumps in the road. You are likely to take a wrong turn here and there. Your efforts are not likely to run without a hitch all the time. So what will keep you going through any rough patches, through the ups and downs of your journey? Nothing less than definiteness of purpose, your dogged determination to get where you want to go. To see every setback as only a temporary defeat giving you pause to reassess and renew your efforts with increased enthusiasm. To stay focused on your million-dollar goal through thick and thin, come what may, with a clear understanding and appreciation that this is part of the process, the refinement if you will, the smoothing out of the edges of your journey as you move yourself ever closer to your goal.

It is those with a definite plan coupled with a definite purpose, who pursue their goal in spite of setbacks, who press on in the face of temporary defeats, understanding that these glitches are part of the process – these are the ones who succeed in life, who in the end are victorious in their pursuit of their dream. If you have a definite plan, a definite goal, a definite objective, and pursue your goals and dreams accordingly, then victory and success will inevitably be yours to relish and enjoy. As you will see in the next chapter, your dominating desires, backed by your definiteness of purpose and definiteness of plans, by universal law, must be manifested in their physical form. In other words, what you focus on with definiteness of purpose, and pursue with unwavering determination, must inevitably come to pass. It cannot be otherwise. It is the way the universe works.

Let me close this chapter by highlighting a few of the principles that you should adopt in pursuit of your goal. We have covered the need for definiteness of purpose and the role it plays in pursuit of your goal. You must master yourself, especially in the area of positive thought. In pursuit of your goal, you cannot afford a single negative, discouraging thought. You must at all times believe in yourself and believe that your goal will be achieved. You must accept temporary setbacks as just that – temporary. Defeat is never permanent unless you make it so. You must find and associate with people who will support and encourage you in the pursuit of your dream. You must think before you act and use your intuition to guide you, to validate your decisions in all things. And, lastly, you must choose your business associates wisely. They must be in complete harmony with your goals and purposes. To choose otherwise would be very harmful to you. Do these things, and success will and must be yours. Do these things, my friend, and you *will* be a millionaire.

Action Item:

1. On a 3x5 index card, write out in bold numbers $1,000,000.

2. Under that number, write the following: I AM OPEN AND ACT UPON THE FASTEST, EASIEST, QUICKEST WAY TO CREATE MY FIRST MILLION DOLLARS.

3. Make yourself three cards. Keep one in your wallet or purse. Put the other two in places where you will see them every day.

4. Read your card at every opportunity, and keep your million-dollar goal in the forefront of your mind. From this day forth, your million-dollar goal is front and center among all your goals until the day you achieve it.

Chapter Four – The Mindset

We are shaped by our thoughts;
we become what we think.

Buddha

Congratulations on making it this far in the book. You must really want to be a millionaire. You have clearly made the decision to be a millionaire. You understand that the main purpose for being a millionaire is to be free to make your unique contribution to the world. And you have set yourself an initial million-dollar goal. Wow! That's a huge change for anybody in such a short amount of time. It's breathtaking. And I'm excited for you. You're doing a great job. Now let's keep going.

Many writers, philosophers, and motivational speakers have shared their belief that our thoughts pretty much give shape to our lives. I used the quote from Buddha at the beginning of this chapter to illustrate that this concept has been around for a long time. Long before we had psychologists and success coaches, there were wise men, thinkers who realized just how powerful our thoughts are, and how they impact and shape our lives.

You have now started thinking about your million-dollar goal. And I have asked you to write it down and keep it in a place where you will see it and read it every day. And in this chapter you will discover just why this is so important.

A mindset consists of the way you think about something. You can have a wealth mindset. You can have a success mindset. Or you can have a poverty mindset. We *choose* the way we think about wealth and abundance (Remember the Goal Card?), just like we *choose* the way we think about lack, scarcity and poverty by accepting it as part of our lives. They are equal in that regardless of the way we choose to think about them or go with this, our subconscious mind takes our thoughts and acts upon them either way regardless.

That is why *how* we choose to think about abundance or lack thereof is so critical to the eventual outcome. This is what having the proper wealth mindset is all about: being focused on abundance, prosperity and in particular a financial goal with a deadline as opposed to being focused on limited resources, scarcity, poverty and lack. Having a proper mindset is a critical part of any measure of success. For the purpose of this book and your goal, we will concern ourselves with a proper wealth mindset.

There are entire books on the subject of becoming what we think about. I prefer to look at this concept a little differently. I see it as we *attract* what we think about. We will cover this in detail in the next chapter. For this chapter, let's consider the individual elements that make up a proper wealth mindset: our thoughts, the level or degree of emotion behind those thoughts, and a sense of worthiness, or deserving to achieve our goal.

Any and all self-made millionaires began their journey with the thought of success. Regardless of their individual circumstances at the time of their decision to be a millionaire, regardless of the difficulties and obstacles they had to overcome in the process of becoming a millionaire, it all began with a thought. That thought turned into a goal, which led to actions necessary to accomplish that goal, which in turn led to their success.

This is why controlling your thoughts is so critically important to the outcome of your success. As I said earlier, control your thoughts, control your life. This means always keep your thoughts positive. In pursuit of your goal, there is no room for thoughts of lack, for thoughts of doubt, worry and fear. There is only room for positive thoughts of anticipation, abundance and success. Granted, this is not always easy to do. But it's now your job to make every effort humanly possible to ward off negative thoughts that might impede your progress and success.

Those negative thoughts may bubble up from within, or they may be lovingly offered by family and friends who may mean well, but are oblivious to what they are actually doing. Wherever they come from and whenever they arise, you must simply take out your magic wand and zap them away. Keep them as far away from your mind as you possibly can. They're deadly and have absolutely no room in your life as a millionaire.

Remember I said your thoughts attract what you think about? This is why you must only think positive thoughts. This not only includes positive thoughts about your goal, it includes positive thoughts about everything. This may seem difficult at first. But I assure you, if you make that effort, it will become a habit and become part of your lifestyle and your new mindset. This includes your thoughts about people, thoughts about life's little inconveniences that can be frustrating and, above all, thoughts about your goal. You must always,

always, always remain positive in all your thoughts.

I think I've made my point on the importance of your thoughts. Along with your thoughts, the second-most important element of your new wealth mindset consists of the emotions you have behind your thoughts. How strongly do you desire to be a millionaire? Is it just something that would be nice if it happens? Or is it something you want as badly as the air you breathe? The degree to which you desire something will largely determine how quickly that something comes into your life. Let me give you a real-life example of how strong emotions behind a fixed desire or goal, coupled with a set deadline by which the goal has to be accomplished, can make things happen that seem miraculous. For me, one particular instance was a matter of life and death.

Not many years ago, I found myself completely out of breath doing the simplest things, like tying my shoes. I suspected something wasn't quite right, so I visited a cardiologist. After a 20-minute examination and a few tests, the doctor informed me that I had a calcified aortic valve. If you remember your biology class, the aortic valve is the large valve of your heart that pumps the blood to the rest of your body. It's pretty important.

Not only was that valve not working properly, but the doctor informed me that it had to be replaced immediately. And if I didn't get it done, his guess was that I had about two weeks to live.

OK, so go get the operation, already. The problem was that I did not have any health insurance at the time. Without health insurance or the money to pay for the operation, the hospital wasn't interested in helping me. It didn't matter that I was dying. That's just the way it is.

So here I am, I need an expensive operation, I need it within two weeks, or I will be dead. This is a great example of a clear goal with a clear timeline and a lot of emotion behind it. That's an understatement. I was going ballistic. Though my wife and I looked far and wide, I couldn't get health insurance because I now clearly had a pre-existing condition. And even if I could get health insurance, there was a 30-day waiting period before benefits could be accessed. I'd be dead in 30 days. What to do?

I knew a solution existed; I just needed access to it. And I was clearly focused on accomplishing just that. As good fortune would have it, the surgeon who would be doing the operation suggested I contact the Larry King Cardiac Foundation. Larry King, who had experienced open-heart surgery himself at the same hospital, no less, had set up a foundation to pay for the surgery for individuals like me who needed it but, for whatever reason, didn't have access to it.

As the clock was ticking, I immediately contacted the foundation and filled out the required paperwork. This was mid-August, and the approving doctors were on their well-deserved vacation. However, as luck would have it, one of the approving doctors returned to his office the last week of August, just before Labor Day. The request was immediately approved. Within hours, I received a call at home from Mrs. King. Once she identified me as the patient in question, she passed the phone over to Larry King. After a few minutes of small talk, Mr. King said to me, "Richard, I understand that you need open-heart surgery. I'm calling to let you know that we will cover the costs of your operation." The man saved my life, and just in the nick of time.

This, I tell my students, is what can happen when you have a clear and definite goal, coupled with a clear and definite deadline, powered by strong emotion and positive thoughts that don't admit or accept defeat, even in the face of death. Like me, you can accomplish miracles. And I fully expect you to.

In addition to your thoughts, and your emotions behind those thoughts, there is a key element to developing a proper wealth mindset that is often overlooked by most people. And that is the component of worthiness.

This may surprise you, but if you don't feel worthy to be a millionaire or to have a million dollars at a gut or visceral level, chances are it just won't happen for you, regardless of how hard you work at it or how great your plans are. That's why this is part of your wealth mindset. You have to be mentally prepared to welcome your newfound wealth with open arms. And for many people, that's not always an easy thing to do.

Consider this. You probably did not grow up in a million-dollar household or spend your summers playing tennis at a country club. Your parents are probably not millionaires. You probably did not personally know any millionaires while you were growing up and probably still don't. And you probably don't pal around with millionaire friends on the weekends. Given these conditions, being a millionaire is probably a bit of a mental stretch for you, which is OK. Like your muscles, your mind can use a little stretching too, even if this exercise represents a *lot* of stretching for you. It's good for you.

So, if you don't already have a sense of worthiness about being a millionaire, how do you cultivate one? Easy. At the end of this chapter, I give you an action item. You will take your Goal cards that you created in the last chapter and you will write two declarations on the back of the cards. In addition to putting your million-dollar goal in your thoughts each day, you will also read these two declarations to yourself daily, preferably twice daily, and preferably aloud.

By absorbing your goal and putting it in the forefront of your thoughts daily, and by then consistently making your two declarations with convincing emotion daily, preferably twice daily, you are literally reprogramming your mind. By focusing on your new wealth mindset day after day, you are not only forming a new personal habit, you are changing your mind as to how you perceive wealth as it pertains to and concerns you.

It generally takes about four to six weeks to form a new habit, especially one that deals with your mental outlook. But after about four to six weeks of doing these daily declarations, you'll notice a subtle change. The change may be more dramatic in some individuals than in others. But all of a sudden, being a millionaire will not feel so strange anymore. Your belief system will start shifting at the very core of your being, at your gut level. Becoming a millionaire will start being more and more believable. You will personally start feeling more and more comfortable with the idea of being a millionaire. You will start experiencing this strange new feeling that becoming a millionaire is entirely possible for you. It is not only possible, it is inevitable. As your excitement grows, so will your confidence. And you will soon be thinking and saying to yourself, "Yes, I can do this. Yes, I deserve this. Yes, this is really happening."

In some literature, the term *hypnotic rhythm* is used to describe actions or thoughts that you consistently entertain and sustain over a period of time. By consistently following through on this daily exercise, you are developing a positive hypnotic rhythm that will confirm, strengthen and reinforce the positive thoughts you are feeding your mind. And, thus, you will be cultivating your new wealth mindset, the mindset of a millionaire.

What are these two declarations, you ask? Simply this:

I **will** be a millionaire by the age of (fill in the blank) or sooner without breaking a sweat.

I **deserve** to be a millionaire by the age of (fill in the blank) or sooner without breaking a sweat.

I add the qualifier 'or sooner' because it may just happen sooner than you expect, depending on how the circumstances in your life play out for you.

And the 'without breaking a sweat' part doesn't mean you won't have to work hard. (By the way, it won't be work. Getting rich is fun.) It simply means that you don't have to worry about the 'how' you're going to get there. Your intuition and the Law of Attraction will guide you to your particular path. This is covered in more detail in the chapters that follow. In the meantime, it's time for you to adopt and cultivate your new wealth mindset. Get to work.

Action Item:

1. On the back of the 3x5 cards that you used to write your million-dollar goal, you will write the following two declarations:

I **will** be a millionaire by the age of (fill in the blank) or sooner without breaking a sweat.

I **deserve** to be a millionaire by the age of (fill in the blank) or sooner without breaking a sweat.

2. Review your goal and make these declarations daily with as much convincing emotion as you can possibly muster.

3. Continue this exercise daily until you become a millionaire.

Chapter Five – The Law of Attraction

What power this is I cannot say.
All that I know is that it exists.

Alexander Graham Bell

...this power of mind is a
universal one, available to the
humblest person as it is to the
greatest.

Andrew Carnegie

I start this chapter with two quotes, instead of one, for a reason. The Law of Attraction, unlike the Law of Gravity, cannot be scientifically proven. However, great thinkers through the ages have not only claimed its existence, but they have attributed much of their success, in large part, to the use of it. The two men quoted above are both extraordinary, and extraordinarily accomplished, by any measure. They were also brilliant men who were not easily duped. They recognized the power of their thoughts, and how their thoughts attracted to them the things they most desired and on which they were most focused.

That power generated by your thoughts, that we call the Law of Attraction today, was formalized in the early 1900s. And today, the concept has become so mainstream, you can find a magazine by that name in the rack at the grocery store.

But I'm not here to convince you that the Law of Attraction exists. I'm telling you that it does, and that it works. This book is living proof of that. I am also telling you that the Law of Attraction will play a central, critical and key role in getting you to your million-dollar goal. You need to understand it, appreciate it and put it to good use. Here's what it is, how it works and how you need to apply it to achieve your million-dollar goal.

A quick note: you will notice similarities among the various moving parts that go into making your goal a reality. Reading this book will help you connect the dots and, like a jigsaw puzzle, will give you the complete picture once all the pieces fall into place. Please be patient.

What is the Law of Attraction? The Law of Attraction is an invisible power much like the Law of Gravity. The Law of Attraction states that you attract to yourself that which you most think about, that which you have the strongest emotions about. This is why you must absolutely be mindful of your thoughts at all times. You attract to yourself what you focus on the most. It doesn't matter what you think about, whether your thoughts are positive in nature or negative, you attract to yourself what you think about. Period.

How does this work? You have both a conscious and a subconscious mind. Your conscious mind is the one through which you experience your current reality, the one created by the use of your five senses and your mind. Your subconscious mind, on the other hand, has no mind of its own. It just takes whatever you think about and works to fulfill your every wish and desire, good or bad. The Law of Attraction is the force that is set in motion by your subconscious mind to bring you that which you think about the most, your dominant desires. That's how it works.

Another way to look at it is that your mind is the boss. It is the creator, the visionary, the one that sets the demands for what you want. Your subconscious mind is your ever-faithful hard-working employee whose only wish is to please the boss and get things done. And the Law of Attraction is the process by which the subconscious mind accomplishes these things.

Now, I could go on to say this 20 different ways to fill up space, but the whole process is really this simple. Once you understand this, you understand the importance of your thoughts and how they affect your life. You must control what you think about. You must manage your emotions. You must shun all negative thoughts like lack of confidence, fear of failure, doubts about your ability to get this million-dollar goal done, and so forth. Monitor your thoughts, paying attention to them at all times. Immediately cancel anything negative and replace it with something positive. Be very sensitive to this. This is important. Negativity has a way of creeping up on you in very subtle ways. You'll get better at this in time. Just make a conscientious effort to only think positive thoughts at all times, as difficult as that may seem at the moment. Make it a habit, and it will become second nature to you.

All self-made millionaires learned this technique early on. They had a goal. They stayed positive in the face of challenges. Like Thomas Edison and the development of the light bulb, they understood that any setbacks or defeats were only temporary, only part of the process. They did not give up. They did not get discouraged. They stayed on task and pursued their dream until it was realized. You will go through the same process to reach your million-dollar goal. You will stay enthusiastically focused on your goal. You will monitor your thoughts to keep them positive at all times. And you will confidently move forward each and every day by taking positive small steps toward your goal.

Another key component of the Law of Attraction is visualization. Visualization is the effort you make to imagine your goal when you think about it daily in exquisite detail, using all five of your senses as much as you possibly can. You feel, see and hear every detail of your life as you can imagine it to be as a millionaire. This, in turn, instructs your subconscious mind to bring your dream reality to you exactly as you have imagined it. It's what professional athletes and actors do before each performance. They visualize what their performance will be like in every detail before they actually do it. Studies show that visualization tricks the subconscious mind into thinking that your thoughts are real. Your subconscious mind does not know the difference between your thoughts and reality. This is why you, as the boss, must give it direction, and not get direction from just any source other than yourself. Visualization is a very powerful and important tool in your wealth arsenal.

As a sense of worthiness is important in cultivating a healthy wealth mindset, it is equally important when it comes to the Law of Attraction. You must be alert, open and welcoming to the signs and signals that come up as you move toward your million-dollar goal. You must genuinely feel that you deserve to be a millionaire. This is the reason you declare this to be true each and every day, and every time you think of your goal. You do this to cancel any negative thoughts you might have lurking within you to the contrary. Think of your TV remote for a moment. You point it at the TV and press a button and the channel changes. Put your hand between the remote and the TV, then press the same button and nothing happens. If you have any negative or restrictive thoughts about being a millionaire, about earning or having a million dollars, then, like your hand between the remote and the TV, you have a block. The Law of Attraction cannot bring to you the things you need to achieve your goal unless this block is removed. Once removed, the power and energy once again freely flow your way.

Have you ever noticed how your energy changes when you get angry or upset about something or someone? Your whole body feels different. And that unsettling feeling lasts until you finally and completely calm down. Notice what kind of energy you're putting out when you feel that way. It's not very good, is it? How do you think it makes the people around you feel? Is that negative energy in any way beneficial? I think not. Negative energy can only hurt you. It will detract you from moving forward on your goal. You simply don't have time for it. Keep it under control and diffuse it whenever it raises its ugly head.

Your new million-dollar goal is probably the most energizing, galvanizing, thought-provoking ambition you have ever had in your life. It is focusing your thoughts in a way your thoughts have never been focused before. Your new goal is changing your motivations, your perceptions, your ambitions, and your creativity in ways that you could scarcely have imagined. In short, your new goal is changing your life for the better, which is what it is meant to do. What an order you are giving to your subconscious mind! What a powerful way to activate the Law of Attraction to bring you all that you need to make your goal a reality!

Keep in mind that the Law of Attraction's process of bringing your goal into reality is not instantaneous. Your subconscious mind has to piece all the different parts of this together for you. Remember that because you're unique, with a unique set of life circumstances, gifts and talents, your path to your million dollars is different from everyone else's. And your subconscious mind has to bring this all together in its proper sequence to make it work for you. Your job is to relax (remember 'without breaking a sweat'?) and stay alert to the signals that come your way. These may come in the form of a brilliant thought, or a feeling about someone or something. Someone will cross your path who may have an interesting idea, or could lead you to someone who could help you. The signs and guideposts will be there. You just need to be alert to them and act upon them when they show up for you.

This is why you absolutely have to stay clear of all negativity. Negativity can only interfere in the process of your developing path. Negativity can only be a barrier to your personal progress when it comes to your financial wealth and well-being. You must be on your guard against this at all times. I cannot emphasize this enough. I know you're tired of hearing me say this. But it's vitally important to your realizing your goal. You want to back away from scarcity and lack and, instead, attract abundance and prosperity. Some people have taken up the habit of carrying a rubber band around their wrist. With this approach, whenever you experience a negative thought, you pull the band and snap your wrist. This serves to jolt you out of your negative thinking and gives you the opportunity to replace your negative thought with a positive one. Do this often enough and your mind will get the message that you do not tolerate negative thoughts.

The Law of Attraction can be summarized in three steps:

1. Think seriously and deeply about your goal.
2. When focusing on your goal, visualize it in as much detail as you can imagine.
3. Be accepting of your goal in that you deserve to achieve it.

Do these things, and your subconscious mind will activate the Law of Attraction to bring you all that you need, in the most efficient manner possible, to make your goal a reality.

To complete this process and leave no stone unturned, take out the pad of paper you had when you made your decision to be a millionaire. Remember the time you took to examine your innermost thoughts about money? Look over your notes and, on a fresh sheet of paper, make a list of all the negative things that may have come up during that exercise. These are your blocks that may prevent the Law of Attraction from operating efficiently in your life to bring you what you need to make your goal a reality. Review these items one at a time. Now write down the opposite of whatever negative money-emotion came up for you. For example, let's say that one of your early negative emotions about money is that "people who are rich are bad people." Then replace that statement with "people who are rich are kind and generous people who help others because they can." Granted, not all rich people are generous and kind. However, as you make your way into those circles, you'll realize that the vast majority of rich people are indeed generous and kind. They are, because they can afford to be – as you will be when you are a millionaire.

Once you've gone through your list of negative thoughts and emotions about money and replaced them with empowering, positive new ones, you will have begun the process of dismantling any block you may have about money and your new goal, and allow the Law of Attraction to work its magic in your life, as it does so well.

Action Item:

1. Pull out the note pad you used to write down you innermost thoughts about money and wealth that may block the Law of Attraction from operating efficiently in your life.

2. For each negative thought about money and wealth that bubbled up for you, write an opposite, positive statement affirming that the opposite is true for you.

3. Keep this list of new thoughts and emotions regarding money and wealth, and review it as often as you can as part of cultivating your new wealth mindset.

4. Continue to review your goal twice daily, and visualize your new life in as much detail as you can possibly imagine.

5. Continue your two daily declarations about your million-dollar goal and the date by which you will achieve it. And continue to affirm your worthiness that you absolutely deserve to achieve your million-dollar goal.

Chapter Six – Intuition

The only real valuable thing is intuition.

Albert Einstein

Let's recap, shall we? You have made the decision to be a millionaire. You understand, and are motivated by, the reason for becoming a millionaire and how becoming a millionaire will change your life. You have a clear goal, which is to create your first $1,000,000. And you have chosen a date by which you will achieve your million-dollar goal. You understand the need to develop and cultivate a wealth mindset by keeping your goal foremost in your thoughts by doing your declarations twice daily, putting some feeling behind your thoughts and declarations, and knowing and accepting that you are worthy and deserve to be a millionaire. And now that you are focused on your goal, you have activated the Law of Attraction that will bring you all that you need to achieve your million-dollar goal. How do you now make sense of all the things that come your way to help you get to your goal? This is where your extraordinary gift of intuition comes into play.

Understand and accept that you have a most extraordinary tool at your disposal as part of your wealth arsenal. More than a compass pointing you in the right direction, your intuition is your gyroscope that will keep you firmly on track toward your goal, regardless of whatever is hurled your way in the process. While your heart and your head can be confounded by emotion and logic, your intuition never misleads you. It is your portal to all the information the Universe has to offer. It is your sixth sense. It can sort through any maze of information, guide you through any set of circumstances, and help you identify all the resources you need to achieve your million-dollar goal. Learn to listen to it.

How does your intuition do this? Your intuition is linked directly to your subconscious mind. That is why we refer to it as your sixth sense. Your intuition lies outside the normal realm of your five senses. In other words, your intuition is not of this world. It is connected to another world far beyond what your five senses can normally pick up, a world that is vast beyond measure, the universal library, if you will. That is why your intuition is able to provide you with information that simply is not available through your head and heart. That is why your intuition is able to sort through for you things that don't yet exist in your world, and why it is able to map out your specific path to your million-dollar goal that is yet to be brought into reality. This is also why your intuition is able to guide you and help you sort through all the things that are provided for you by way of the Law of Attraction, which you have unleashed by focusing on your million-dollar goal.

Now that you have activated the Law of Attraction to bring you all the things you need to accomplish your million-dollar goal, your intuition is there to help you sort it all out. As you ponder your goal and search for your path to get there, thoughts and feelings about things and people will suddenly come to you. Take note of them. Filter them through your intuition. Do they feel right? Should you look into a particular business idea? Should you contact a particular person? Let your intuition guide you as to the appropriateness of these things. If something comes up that doesn't seem to make sense on the surface, but feels right by way of your intuition, go with your intuition. It may just be that the benefit of a particular thing or person is not the thing or person itself, but the connection it provides to something or someone else that you really need. That is how the Law of Attraction works.

I have experienced this connectivity of things over and over again in my life. I put my efforts out in one direction because I feel strongly about it and it seems right at the time, only to be led by circumstances to something entirely different. This book is a prime example of this phenomenon. I started out with an entirely different project in mind. I paid a lot of money to attend a conference to help me develop that idea. Though I received confirmation from many that I had a good idea, I just couldn't seem to make it happen. However, the contacts and connections I made by attending that conference have led me to *The Student Millionaire* project, and to the book that you are reading today. The lesson learned is that you have to trust the intuitive process and get out of your own way so it can happen. Let your intuition be your guide.

Remember, your path to your million-dollar goal is unique to you. As I state in the beginning of the book, on the whole planet Earth, there does not exist an exact duplicate of you – someone who looks like you, has your personality, your particular set of skills, talents and gifts, and your life circumstances. There is only one you. In this entire world, you are unique. And because of your uniqueness and all the unique aspects of your life, your path to your million-dollar goal is equally uniquely yours.

There may be similarities between your path and someone else's, but your paths will not be the same. They cannot be. Your world is different from everyone else's. And so is your path to your million-dollar goal.

Now, your intuition is usually pretty quick with an answer, especially when the question is simple. But your million-dollar goal is a little more complex than a simple question. By asking the question, "What is the fastest, easiest, quickest way for me to create my first million dollars?" you are really challenging your subconscious mind to work overtime and have the Law of Attraction bring into your life all that you need to make this happen. That's a complex question. A lot of sorting out has to take place here. The Universe has to take into account a wide range of things. It weighs your thoughts on the subject, and how much emotion or desire you put behind those thoughts. It considers your interests, your talents, gifts and abilities. It sorts through your life circumstances to see who you know and what contacts can be made. It develops a custom-made plan just for you for the best, most efficient way for you to reach your million-dollar goal. And like a GPS, it self-corrects along the way. You just have to stay tuned in.

Now all of this will take a little time to sort out. There's a lot to sort out, so that the fastest, quickest, easiest way for you to get to your million-dollar goal is laid out for you. As frustrating as it may be, not all the answers will be laid in front of you at the beginning of your journey. This is where you have to have a little trust and faith in yourself. Believe that you can do this. Believe that this is possible for you. And believe that, as sure as night turns to day, this will happen for you. You will be a millionaire.

It's important to remember and appreciate the fact that, as a young adult, you probably have not had the benefit of extensive training in business or much experience as an entrepreneur. And here you are setting your sights on a million-dollar goal. How crazy is that? It's not. It's awesome. The Universe is waiting for you to get started. You have given your subconscious mind the order. And the wheels of your request have been set in motion. Since you don't have the benefit of experience or training to do this, you have to rely on your intuition to guide you along your path. We'll discuss the benefits of finding and working with a real-life Mentor in the last chapter of the book.

The answers will come in pieces, one at a time, and they always come at just the right time. Your job is to be alert and open to them. Whether it comes as a thought, a person, a feeling about something or someone who just happens to cross your path, you can be sure of one thing: that the pieces are all interconnected, that they all follow the Universe's logic, not yours, and that they are perfectly sequential in the order that they need to be for you to reach your million-dollar goal. Besides, this is your custom-made plan, isn't it? You cannot ask for a better business partner, trainer, teacher or coach, one who has your back and is watching out for you, than your intuition. It will not fail you.

Don't worry. You'll get better at tapping into your intuition. The more you use, rely on, and trust your intuition, the better you'll get at making use of it to get to where you want to go. I know this is a lot to absorb the first time around. Be patient. It will all come together, I promise. And the way it comes together will simply astound you. As you stay focused on your million-dollar goal, the people who will cross your path, the things that will start happening to you, the inspiring thoughts you will have, will all seem to be coming out of nowhere. They're coming from somewhere. They're just not coming from the world you know.

A word of caution: Sometimes, what may seem like intuition isn't. It may be a strong first impression that is based on your particular, individual set of past experiences. Not to worry. The more you practice and use your intuition, the more you will grow to recognize the difference between strong impressions and what your intuition is really telling you. If you make a mistake once in a while, and misjudge or misinterpret the feelings about something, don't fret. This will happen once in a while. Just keep in mind that the vast majority of the time, you will be correct in following what your intuition is directing you to do. This has worked like magic for thousands of years. It is not about to change anytime soon.

As you embark upon this journey, remember to be kind to yourself. Give yourself the gift of reflection. Give yourself the time to think. Don't rush and hurry all the time. Yes, there will be deadlines to meet. But short of that, just give yourself time to think about the things to which you are seeking answers. Remember back when you took the time to meditate on your possible money and wealth issues? You thought about it for a few minutes, and then proceeded to write down everything that came to mind. You actually took the time to do that. Take the time to do the same for your million-dollar goal. Schedule or set aside some time to just think about it. You can sit down with a pad of paper like you did when you made your decision to be a millionaire, or you can just go for a walk. The important thing is that you take the time to do this, to reflect on your million-dollar goal and on the best way to get yourself there. Think about your next steps, about what decisions you have to make. See what comes up. Maybe nothing. Maybe just one prompting, thought or feeling about something. Whatever it is, pay attention to it. Does it feel right? Is it something you've been thinking about, or is it something brand new? Don't judge it with your head or your heart.

Filter it through your intuition. And take the time to do this on a regular basis. This is an opportunity for you to listen to your intuition, to open yourself up to that vast universal storehouse of information. Your intuition is just an amazing resource. Learn to make your intuition your best friend. Learn to make of use it.

Action Item:

1. Practice, practice, practice.

This is the best way to develop your expertise at using your intuition. As often as you can in the course of the day, or as often as you can remember to do this, get in touch with how you feel about something. Check yourself to see if that something feels right, or if that something doesn't feel quite right. This is the skill that you need to cultivate and develop, in order to pick up on the signals and guideposts your intuition will be sending you as you move toward your million-dollar goal. Keep doing this as often as you can, and I assure you that you will become quite proficient in discerning when your intuition is trying to tell you something that you need to know or to do.

Chapter Seven – The Money Rules

*One penny may seem to you a
very insignificant thing, but it is
the small seed from which
fortunes spring.*

Orison Swett Marden

The quote above, by Orison Swett Marden, was written by a man who was orphaned at age 7, raised in foster homes as an indentured servant, worked his way through college, became a lawyer and a doctor, owned hotels and other businesses, lost it all in the depression of the 1890s, and started all over again. He knew the value of money. More importantly, he knew the value of personal development and self-control.

This book lays out a path for your journey to wealth. You will note that 80% of the path depends on your personal development, what happens internally – your decision, your mindset, your courage, persistence and focus. Also critical to being wealthy is the ability to manage your money – the other 20%. We've all heard stories of rich athletes and lottery winners who end up broke. What happened to all that money? Clearly, these folks could have used some instruction in financial literacy. It's one thing to have money. It's another to know how to manage it and hang on to it. Yes, you can hire people to do that for you. But it's your money. You should have some idea of how to manage it and what your options are.

We can't cover all you need to know about managing your money in one chapter. That's why you'll find a list of recommended books at the end of this book. I hope you will continue your financial education far beyond *The Student Millionaire*. What we will cover in this chapter are a few basic, principal money rules that everyone should know and follow, some of which have been around for millennia.

Money is a game. And, like all games, it has rules. Most people don't even realize they are playing the game. And even fewer know the rulebook on how to succeed and win the game. The reason the rich get richer is that they know they are in the game and they play by the rules.

Rule No. 1: Save at Least 10% of Every Dollar Received.

The #1 rule you and everyone else need to start playing by is to save at least 10% of every dollar you receive. Simple enough, but who follows it? Most adults are in the habit of paying their bills first – the mortgage, groceries, utilities and cable. Then, after the bills are paid, they check to see if there is anything left to save. More often than not, there isn't. And so it goes through the years. There's never a cushion for emergencies, nor are there any savings when retirement rolls around. This is a recipe for disaster.

You, on the other hand, have the most valuable asset needed when it comes to creating wealth – time. Even if you did nothing else but follow this rule from this day forward for the rest of your working career, you would be infinitely better off when you retire than 95% of the American public. The key here is consistency. Develop the habit early, as in *now*, to save 10% of every dollar you earn and receive, and stick to it forever. This includes ALL dollars received, including all cash gifts. Warren Buffet said it best: don't save after you spend, spend after you save.

What would add icing to your savings cake is to find a place to put your savings where you earn 5 to 10% annual interest, compounding yearly, on your money. Compound interest alone would be the difference between having a few hundred thousand dollars in 40 years in your savings account, and a couple million dollars for retirement. In today's economy, this is not an easy thing to find. But you might want to keep this on your radar screen and on your to-do list, as you keep moving toward your million-dollar goal.

Rule No. 2: Practice Charitable Giving.

The principle of charitable giving is as old as time. Tithing, which is giving 10% of your income to charity, is referenced in the Old Testament in Malachi 3:10. In Hinduism and Buddhism, dāna is the practice of cultivating generosity through giving. In Islam, zakāt, the giving of a portion of one's wealth, is one of the Five Pillars of Muslim life.

There are several reasons why one should give a portion of one's earnings. One reason is that it helps people. Americans give billions of dollars a year to charity and nonprofit organizations that benefit millions of people. Would the world still exist if we didn't do that? Of course. But the world is a much better place because so many people are generous. And remember, your purpose for becoming a millionaire is to be able to make your unique contribution to the world, whatever that may be.

Another reason for giving at least a portion of your earnings and, in your case, your wealth, is very much in line with your new wealth mindset of prosperity and abundance. People who say they can't afford to give have a lack, scarcity, and poverty mindset. They fear that, by being charitable, they will not have enough for themselves. That kind of mindset, if you understand the Law of Attraction, will only bring them more scarcity and lack. Giving is definitely in line with a millionaire mindset. Do not fear to be generous. It is great training as you cultivate your newfound wealth mindset.

Rule No. 3: Monitor Your Expenses.

Unfortunately, this is where many adults fail miserably. Many adults, once they get paid, are in the habit of paying their bills, buying a Starbucks coffee on the way to work every day, buying lunch every day instead of bringing their own, and spending on whatever else comes up in the course of life. Few families actually live by a budget and monitor their expenses to see where all the money goes.

In addition to developing the habit of saving 10% of all you earn and receive, and setting a portion aside for charitable giving as an exercise in developing your wealth mindset, it is critically important that you monitor and do everything you can to minimize your expenses. If you have to, keep a pocket notebook to track your spending habits for a week. Then, take a good hard look and see if you could have maybe spent your money a little differently. As you build your wealth, it is critically important to minimize your expenses, save your money, and invest in things that will earn you money in the future. You'll understand this better as you move along toward your million-dollar goal.

Let me tell you about Oseola McCarty. Back in the 1990s, Miss McCarty made national headlines when she generously donated a cash gift of $150,000 to the University of Southern Mississippi to help poor students pay their tuition. Many wealthy people give larger gifts to universities and never make the news. What made Miss McCarty's gift so extraordinary was the fact that she was a poor, old-fashioned laundress with a 6th-grade education who never earned more than $10 for a bundle of laundry all her working life. When asked about her secret for being able to make such a gift, Miss McCarty answered, "I lived simply. I saved whatever I could and I never touched it!" What an extraordinary example of the power of saving and monitoring your expenses!

Rule No. 4: Protect Your Money.

Guard your money with your life. Remember the earlier reference about wealthy athletes and lottery winners going broke? They clearly did not protect their money. They clearly did not save anything, and clearly did not monitor their expenses.

Resist the temptation to buy new and expensive stuff on credit. You buy new and expensive stuff when your investments earn you enough money to do so. That way, you're not paying the bank just to be able to buy your new and expensive stuff. And you're not hurting yourself financially either, because your investments will continue to provide you with money even after you make your purchases. For example, as you work your way toward your million-dollar goal and need a car, you buy a good used car that is less than five years old, has less than 50,000 miles, and is good on gas. This will serve you just fine for the time you need it. You save on the car payments. You save on the interest that you pay on those payments. And you demonstrate an aptitude for managing your money well.

Is this hard? For a lot of people, it is. There is so much pressure from family and friends, and society as a whole, to put on a good show. But putting on a good show when you can't afford it will keep you from becoming rich. That's why you have to remain steadfast on your million-dollar goal, and not get sidetracked by things that will pull you away from it. This is called delayed gratification. And it is especially hard to swallow when you're young. You want to be able to enjoy the best life has to offer. And no one can blame you for that. But you have to learn to manage your emotions and desires. Harness them and use them to your own advantage to focus on your million-dollar goal. And, soon enough, you will be able to enjoy the fruits of your labor.

Rule No. 5: Own Your Own Home.

Either way you look at it, it costs to buy a home and it costs to maintain a home. But in the end, you at least own something that has value that, with some effort, can be turned into cash. You cannot turn your apartment into cash if you're only renting it. You cannot put your apartment on your balance sheet as being an asset with a market value. Some would argue that a home is not an asset because it does not generate income. Be that as it may, it is still better to own your own home than it is to rent.

One of the best things you can do is add real estate to your wealth arsenal. And you can start doing that by reading up on how you go about buying your first place. There's an excellent book on the subject at the end of this book. Real estate is valuable because it will never be worth zero dollars. Unlike stocks in companies that crash and burn, real estate has always been, and will always be, one area on which to focus your investments.

Once you own your own home, you might want to venture out into the rental property business, either by yourself or with a partner. Some people have no interest in real estate beyond owning their own home. However, if your intuition tells you that real estate is for you, you will have an excellent vehicle by which, and through which, you can reach your million-dollar goal.

Rule No. 6: Plan for the Future.

By latching on to your million-dollar goal and your goal to be a millionaire, you are clearly planning for the future. Truth of the matter is that most people don't plan for their financial future. About 60% of today's retirees have little or no retirement savings. They rely totally on Social Security and the generosity of family and friends. They didn't intend for things to turn out that way. They just got carried away with life and neglected to plan accordingly.

But you won't let that happen to you, right? You are planning and working toward being not only financially self-sufficient. You are planning on being downright wealthy. You're planning on being a millionaire. And you are staying focused on that goal until you reach it.

By virtue of your million-dollar goal, you have this part of your life covered. By focusing on your goal, you will be more focused on investments and owning your own business and creating income-generating assets, rather than being focused on spending what you earn today.

Rule No. 7: Expand Your Wealthability.

This is just a cute way of saying that you need to continue your lifelong journey of wealth creation by continuing your lifelong interest in learning, especially learning about finances and investments. Read books. Take classes and courses. Attend lectures and seminars. Become friends with financially successful people that you want to emulate, and with whom you want to associate. In short, put learning about wealth on your daily radar screen and keep it there permanently.

You have your million-dollar goal. And you have your purpose that motivates you to achieve that goal. You know how to cultivate a wealth mindset. And you know how the Law of Attraction and your intuition work to help get you to your goal. Adopt and follow these money rules and, in no time, you will start seeing tangible results from your efforts.

Is it simple? Yes. Is it easy? No. The wealth process requires dedication and commitment. It requires self-discipline and hard work. Is it worth it? Absolutely! There is no price too great to pay for freedom, especially financial freedom. With a slight tweak in attitude, your hard work can be turned into a labor of love. You'll only be working for yourself. Just learn the rules.

Action Item:

1. If you don't already have one, open up a savings account at your local bank or credit union. Ask about fees and minimum balances. Remember, this is a *savings* account. Make it hard to get to. Do not ask for or accept an ATM card or companion checking account for your savings account. This is where you will squirrel away your 10% and keep adding to it forever. Stay alert to ways you can increase the interest you earn.

2. Start giving some thought to what charities you might support with that part of your income.

3. Monitor your spending. Get a pocket notebook and keep track of your spending for a week. Review it. It will probably be quite revealing.

4. Finish this book. When you're done, spend some time thinking about what you have learned. Then find ways to continue your financial education by attacking the list of recommended books you will find at the end of this book.

Chapter Eight – Believing

*Magic is believing in yourself, if
you can do that, you can make
anything happen.*

Johann Wolfgang von Goethe

Believing is such a central, critical and key component of success, that it deserves its own chapter.

What do you think of your journey so far? If you're like most young adults, it should be quite an eye opener. You've not only made the definite decision to be a millionaire, you've learned how that goal and your thoughts about that goal set the wheels in motion to bring you all that you need to achieve it. And the glue that holds all of this together is believing in yourself.

You have set yourself a goal of earning, making, creating $1,000,000 for yourself. And you have given yourself a deadline, a date by which you will achieve that, and by which you will make that happen. By any stretch of the imagination, that goal is breathtaking. And it's doable. More importantly, it's doable by you. Thousands do it every year. So why not you? What's different between those who achieve a million dollars for themselves and you? Nothing. They believe in themselves, and so should you.

The bottom line here is that you have all you need to get yourself there. You are smart enough. You are talented enough. You are resourceful enough. And you know enough people to get you started. I can tell you these things, but you have to believe them yourself. I can just imagine what some of you are thinking right now. "I want to get there, but I haven't got a clue on how to get there or on what to do to get there."

Excuse me, but remember the part about the Mindset, the Law of Attraction, and your Intuition? You're focusing on your goal every day. And while you're doing that, you're listening to your intuition for clues on what direction to take and on what actions to take in that direction to move you toward your goal. Don't forget that your sixth sense, your intuition, is tapping into the universal library to find the best way, the fastest way, and the easiest way for you to get there. It's a process. Just be patient.

Your job is to continue to focus on your goal every day without fail. Listen and pay attention to the signs and clues you get, such as thoughts and impressions. What is your intuition telling you? Stay focused on your goal and let the Law of Attraction do its work. And the key to making all this work is believing in yourself.

I know that believing in yourself is often easier said than done. A million-dollar goal is a huge shift in mindset for anyone, especially a young adult like you. I know. It was for me, as well, even as an older adult. But I have my results to prove to you that these principles work. Again, this book is one prime example of the application of these principles.

Remember when we were discussing how to develop and cultivate a new wealth mindset? You started by declaring your goal twice daily, along with the date by which you will achieve your goal. Along with the declaration of your goal, you added a second declaration affirming your sense of worthiness, in that you really deserve to be a millionaire. I also indicated that it normally takes about four to six weeks for these declarations to start taking effect, before you start believing them, and before they work their way into your core set of beliefs.

Give yourself the gift of these two simple daily declarations and the 4 to 6 weeks it takes for these to take hold. Notice how your feelings about being a millionaire begin to change over this time frame. When you start doing this, it is probably very difficult, even uncomfortable, not only to think of yourself as a millionaire, but to think that being a millionaire is even possible for you. How crazy is that? But as the weeks go by and you continue your two declarations daily, which include keeping your million-dollar goal on your radar screen, you begin to feel different. All of a sudden, the thought of being a millionaire doesn't seem so strange anymore. All of a sudden, you start thinking that being a millionaire really is possible for you. And, most importantly, all of a sudden, you start believing that, yes, you can really do this thing. You can really achieve your million-dollar goal. And you begin to see how you will do it. You are successfully reprogramming your mind into a new wealth mindset. And the more you fill in the details, the more you grow in confidence and the realization that you have indeed put yourself on the path to becoming a millionaire. You now believe in yourself.

This is exciting. You've never felt this way before, certainly not about anything like this. Me? A millionaire? How cool is that? Yes, it is very cool. And to make sure you don't get sidetracked, you must be very mindful of your thoughts at all times. They must always be positive. You must shun any doubts about your abilities to do this. (Have faith in yourself.) You must dispel any worries you might have about how you're going to get this done. (Know that your intuition will reveal your particular path to you.) And you must face any fears you might have about how being a millionaire might change your life.

This includes the opinions and thoughts of people around you who may not think the way you are now thinking. How do you deal with someone you love, admire and respect, who tells you that this million-dollar goal of yours is a fantasy? "Get real. Get a real job like everybody else. And forget this millionaire nonsense." What do you do? How do you handle this? This is when you do what every great person before you has done at a time like this – you simply believe in yourself.

You believe in yourself by doing the things that I have taught you in this book. You focus on your goal each and every day. You focus on your deadline by which you will achieve that goal. You affirm your worthiness to achieve your goal. And you take note each and every day of the signs and signals the Law of Attraction provides for you to get you there. You stay on course. You don't deviate. You don't worry about the how. You let your intuition act as your gyroscope, as it keeps you on track to achieve your goal. And you just keep moving forward. And by doing these things, you will inevitably reach your million-dollar goal. You have to believe.

Is this process easy? Not always. Just like your goal is inevitable if you stay focused and consistent, negative thoughts of fear, worry, and self-doubt are also inevitable. They are part of human nature, the left-brain part, to be exact. Your left brain represents the logical you, the one that tries to make sense of everything. Its job is to protect you and try to keep you from causing harm to yourself. Since being a millionaire is a new concept with which your brain is unfamiliar and you don't know exactly how you are going to get there, the logical part of you will not know how to handle this new leap into uncharted territory. Red flags and flashing lights are bound to pop up everywhere. WARNING! WARNING! YOU ARE VENTURING INTO UNCHARTED WATERS. TO BE SAFE, IT IS BETTER TO TURN BACK AND AVOID THEM ALTOGETHER!!!

This will come up in many different ways. It will come up as the fear to assert yourself to move forward in this direction. It will manifest itself in the form of doubts that you could possibly be capable enough to ever pull this off, or that this could even possibly be done. Or worse, you could have an anxiety attack that you might even be successful at pulling this off. What then? What will people think of you? How will this change your life? Could your family and friends handle it? Could you handle it?

These and a myriad of other negative thoughts are likely to come up. And this could be quite scary. How do you handle them when they do raise their ugly heads? You must remember where they are coming from. This is your left brain talking. Its job is to make sense of reality and keep you safe. It doesn't understand things like faith, belief, and intuition. Your right brain is the home of these things. Faith and intuition are foreign concepts to your left brain. So be polite and just tell your left brain, "Thanks for sharing. But I prefer to remain positive and move forward toward my goal and with my life. Thank you very much. Now go away!"

Acknowledge these thoughts when they come up and consciously let them go. Choose to make the effort to think differently. These negative thoughts are of no use to you. Let them go as quickly as they come to you. By practicing this habit, you will notice that, over time, the frequency of these thoughts will diminish to the point that they will rarely ever come up again. You will be developing what Napoleon Hill calls the Law of Hypnotic Rhythm. This Law applies to your thoughts and actions as you repeat them over a period of time. Like your subconscious mind, this Law doesn't care whether your thoughts or actions are positive or negative. It will just get you in the rhythm of whichever one you choose. That is why you must choose wisely. You must always choose to be positive, and always choose positive thoughts that move you in the direction of your goal.

It is important to understand that your thoughts and your mind are the only things over which you truly have complete and unequivocal control. Let me say this again. There is nothing else in your life over which you have total and absolute control, other than your thoughts and your mind. That is why your mind is truly what you make of it. And this, in turn, is why your life is what you make of it. Control your thoughts and you will control your life. It's that simple.

This is a huge part of believing in yourself. We have seen how the subconscious mind takes your thoughts and, like the ever-faithful employee, does whatever is necessary to fulfill your thoughts and desires. It doesn't judge whether these thoughts are positive or negative, whether these thoughts are beneficial or harmful to you. It just does what you tell it to do by the thoughts you hold foremost in your mind. Again, this is the critical importance of staying steadfast in your positive thoughts.

As you go through the process starting from where you are today to achieving your million-dollar goal, there will be many ups and downs. Remember that none of them are permanent. Successes are not permanent. Defeats or setbacks are not permanent. They are all just part of the process. Please understand that, and remember this as your path to your million-dollar goal unfolds. Learn to appreciate and recognize the process for what it is – a process. Stay positive and continue to believe in yourself and in the process at all times, and you will be victorious.

Imagine yourself having started with nothing, staying positive, diligent and steadfast in your journey to your million-dollar goal and getting there. Imagine yourself looking back at all the ups and downs you experienced in the process, and never losing faith in yourself, nor doubting that you would eventually reach your goal. Imagine the enormous satisfaction you feel at having accomplished this amazing thing when you had no reason to, except that you believed in yourself. This, my friend, is what you have to look forward to when you cross the finish line, achieve your million-dollar goal, and join the millionaire club. You did it, and were able to do it because, first and foremost, you believed in yourself and never wavered from that belief.

I believe in you. I believe that you can do this. And I will relish every bit of your story that you share with me when you get there. See you at the finish line.

Action Item:

1. Keeping your $1,000,000 goal in front of you, continue your two declarations daily without fail: You will be a millionaire by a date of your choosing, and you deserve to be a millionaire. Do this each and every day, and continue strengthening your wealth mindset.

Chapter Nine – Courage & Confidence

We gain strength, and courage,
and confidence by each
experience in which we really
stop to look fear in the face... we
must do that which we think we
cannot.

Eleanor Roosevelt

All right then, you have made your decision to be a millionaire. And you understand the real reasons to be a millionaire: beyond the money, it is to be the person you were meant to be, to live the life you were born to live, and to make the unique contribution to the world that only you can make. This is your true motivation that will carry you through times when things may not be going quite as you had planned.

Knowing this, you are beginning your wealth journey by setting yourself an initial goal of $1,000,000. You understand the millionaire mindset, that this is a must for you to achieve this million-dollar goal. And each day, you get better and better at relying on your intuition as your guide through this whole process.

And, finally, you really and truly believe that you can do this, that this can really happen for you and that you will indeed be a millionaire. Congratulations! You are on your way.

In the course of reading your way to this point, you may remember several references to the likelihood of negative thoughts raising their ugly heads. And, like the mythic Hydra, no sooner have you dispelled one, two others will appear. This is normal. You have to get used to it. Just know that in time, they will not only diminish, they will disappear entirely. You just have to give it time and keep working at dispelling them.

Just by giving yourself a million-dollar goal and reading this book, you have displayed extraordinary courage by being willing to break away from the pack and charting a new course for yourself. You have decided to take control of your thoughts and think for yourself. And, by doing so, you have taken control of your life.

You have every reason to be very proud of yourself for doing this. At the moment, only two out of a hundred people would do this. Let's see if we can increase that number, shall we?

The courage you have demonstrated by embarking on this journey and putting yourself on the path to wealth must now become a permanent fixture in the make-up of your character. Courage must now become your middle name. It will take courage to continue on this path until you achieve your million-dollar goal. It will take courage to continue believing in yourself, even when you have no apparent reason to, except that you desire to achieve this goal more than anything else. It will take courage to stick to your goal as you navigate your way through your family and friends, who do not understand the decision you have made for yourself, much less the process you are going through to get yourself to your goal. And you will need courage to continue to believe in yourself as you increasingly need to rely on yourself, your thoughts and your intuition to navigate the different elements of your million-dollar journey.

The path that unfolds before you may be very different from the one you originally envisioned. Remember, that one came from your thoughts. The path you are putting yourself on will be custom-designed for you, based on your overriding million-dollar goal. Your intuition will be your guide through all that your subconscious mind and the Law of Attraction bring your way. As strange as this may seem to you, this is how it works.

And as your path unfolds before you, it will take courage for you to get out of your own way and listen to your intuition. It is not that you are right or wrong, it is just that your intuition has access to vastly more resources and information than you do. In our physical world, we have access to limited resources. And our brain can only make sense of what we can interpret through our five senses. Our intuition, on the other hand, is our sixth sense, our portal to all that the universe has to offer. We have to believe in ourselves enough to trust it, let it guide us, and listen to what it is telling us.

I am combining the quality of confidence with the attribute of courage, because believing in yourself requires you to be sure of yourself. Self-confidence is the quality that gives you the courage to believe in yourself, that gives you the courage to do the things you have to do, that gives you the courage to trust yourself. Self-confidence must be as much a part of who you are as courageous, to get yourself through the process you are undertaking.

Self-confidence will get you started and will sustain you until you reach your goal. This is fine intellectually. But how do you develop self-confidence if you don't exactly have it in abundance at the moment?

You start with your daily declarations. You affirm your million-dollar goal daily and affirm that you will be a millionaire. You affirm daily that you are worthy to achieve your million-dollar goal, that you fully and absolutely deserve to be a millionaire. As you do this, the idea of becoming a millionaire becomes less and less strange, and you become more and more confident in your abilities to get this done. In other words, you grow in confidence.

And, as you grow in confidence, you are better able to shrug off the fears and doubts that will inevitably crop up. You can stare them down and blow them off. You're in charge. You're doing this. And you will let nothing sidetrack you. Confidence will give you the strength to fight any doubts you may have about doing this, about your abilities to do this, and about your ability to get this done. End of story.

In addition to your daily declarations (Remember, daily means daily, as in every day without fail until you reach your goal, however long it takes. Understand?

Another technique you can use to increase your self-confidence is visualization. Visualization is the process by which you visualize the outcome of your million-dollar goal in as much detail as you can possibly muster.

You think about what your life will be like after you become a millionaire. Who you will be hanging around with? What you will be doing? What is the first thing you want to do, or buy, when you make your first million dollars? Just think about it.

Take the time to dream and visualize what your life will be like. How different is it from the life you are living today? How different is it from the life you would be living if you were not a millionaire? As you think about these details and imagine how your life will be, you are feeding these thoughts to your subconscious mind. You are holding these thoughts in your mind with positive emotions and energy. Therefore, you are including them in the mix along with your overriding million-dollar goal. And by doing so, you are again setting the wheels in motion for the Law of Attraction to bring you that which you desire, that on which you focus the most. Amazing how it continues to all fit together, isn't it?

And while you're thinking about this, try another technique to implant your future in your mind. Take a few minutes to write a narrative of the future you envision. But write it out using the present tense. That is, write it as if you were living that life today. By doing so, you are conveying to your subconscious mind that your goals have already been achieved. This helps the Law of Attraction bring what you are imagining to you more quickly. And as the results of your thoughts and actions begin to materialize before your very eyes, your confidence will soar. You will know that you really are able to do this, that you are really the one making this happen.

Remember that your intuition will direct you to and line your path to the million-dollar goal that is specific to you. In mapping out your custom-made plan to your million-dollar goal, the universe, with its infinite wisdom and array of combinations of people, events and resources, will take into account your personality. Though personalities can be classified into a few categories, your personality type will be accounted for in your path to your million-dollar goal. A shy person will not likely be put in sales. An outgoing type-A personality is not likely to be given a path where the personality is not given the opportunity to shine. Your path is tailor-made for you. And your intuition will reveal this to you early on as you begin your journey.

Another important thing that increases your confidence when it comes to creating wealth is knowledge: knowledge about your business, and knowledge about financial literacy, specifically in the areas that pertain to your particular enterprise, business and path. Knowledge and training can both prevent you from the many pitfalls that you would otherwise experience, and accelerate the attainment of your goal. Whatever line of work or enterprise you are led to, think about ways you might increase your knowledge about what you are doing. Check in with your intuition. Who should you be talking to? What training is available for your particular line of work? How can you get better, more efficient and more effective at what you do? How can you accelerate your personal and business development? The answers to these and other questions will be enormously beneficial and helpful to you as you make your way to your million-dollar goal.

You cannot be happy, nor can you make a lot of money, unless you believe in yourself. Period. That's the long and short of it. Once you understand and accept this statement as true, you will marvel at the things you will dare to do and accomplish. And you will do these things because you realize that doing these things doesn't depend on others. They depend on you, and you alone. And one of the main things this belief in yourself, this self-confidence, does is that it dispels the fears that keep you from doing them. Fears allow obstacles to block your path. Self-confidence allows you to bulldoze your way through these fears, these obstacles, and get on with what you have to do to get to your million-dollar goal.

The people who accomplish things are the people who have self-confidence. If you hold your million-dollar goal in the forefront of your mind each and every day, and you do your two declarations with conviction each and every day, affirming your goal and your worthiness to achieve it, your confidence will grow with you and increase every day. If you follow that by doing what your intuition instructs you to do to move yourself toward your goal, and you do so with ever increasing confidence, you cannot help but accomplish what you set out to do. This is the amazing formula with which we are dealing. This is the formula by which you will become a millionaire.

Let's take a look at some basic principles we've covered along the way. You know that you have the ability to accomplish anything that you undertake. With your newfound and ever-strengthening wealth mindset, you know that whatever you think about long enough, and with sufficient emotion, will materialize into your reality. You know that by focusing on your goal, you are attracting everything you need to accomplish that goal. You know that, as your path crystallizes, you will either need to acquire new knowledge to accomplish the things you need to do, or you will find people with the expertise you need to get it done. But stay focused and you *will* get it done.

As we bring this chapter to a close, you know that the killer of innumerable dreams is negative thinking in the form of fear, doubts, worries and concerns. You know that you must consciously avoid these negative energies like the plague. Make every effort to dispel them, cancel them, and replace them with their positive and beneficial counterparts. This will do wonders to keep you on track, keep you focused, and greatly facilitate the accomplishment of your million-dollar goal.

I would like to suggest one last exercise to jolt you into believing in yourself and build the necessary confidence and courage you will need to accomplish your goal. Do your daily declarations with conviction in front of a mirror and look yourself directly in the eye. Tell that person, in no uncertain terms, that you will be a millionaire by a date of your choosing without breaking a sweat. Look at that person you see in the mirror and tell that person that they deserve to be a millionaire in no uncertain terms. Not only do they deserve to be a millionaire, but that they are totally, completely and absolutely worthy of becoming a millionaire.

By doing this in front of a mirror and looking yourself directly in the eye, you are jolting your subconscious mind into accepting these statements as true, and giving it the order to get to work for you and make it happen. Yes, it will be awkward at first. It will take some getting used to. But do it day after day and notice the change in yourself. Notice your increased confidence in going about making your goal happen. Notice your increased courage to speak to people, the thought of which would have scared you to death in the past. Take note of the new you, the evolving you. You are really quite remarkable. You will notice the change in yourself, and so will the people around you. They will be so impressed with the new you. You will be impressed with the new you.

You have come such a long way from the person who opened this book and started reading Chapter One, not sure of what you would find. By reading this book, you have discovered the power of your mind, the power of your thoughts. You now know that by controlling your thoughts, you control your mind. And by controlling your mind, you control your life. And this knowledge will serve you well for as long as you shall live.

Chapter Ten – The Business

*Effort only fully releases its
reward after a person refuses to
quit.*

Napoleon Hill

So here we are at the end or, more appropriately, at the beginning for you. I'm saddened that, with this chapter, we are bringing our journey together to a close. However, like a parent who dusts off the wings of his child in preparation for the flight ahead, my heart is so full of eager anticipation for you. You have been given an extraordinary set of tools which, if you take them to heart, will absolutely transform your life.

Now it's up to you. It's up to you to use these tools to design and create the exact life you want.

What will it be? You need to give yourself the gift of time to think about that question. Take out your trusty pad and pen, and start writing down the different elements that, for you, make up the ideal life. Keep doing that until a picture emerges that you know represents your ideal life. Make it a part of your daily goals. Keep it in your thoughts every day.

Now, to make that life a reality, you're going to need money. Teaching you to create and attract that money into your life is the purpose of this book and the reason you have spent the time reading it. I've said repeatedly that your path to your million-dollar goal is unique to you. Your path may have elements that are similar to other people's paths. But, like snowflakes, no two paths are exactly alike.

Once you get a handle on what your ideal life looks like, do the same for your particular path to wealth. This is not likely to come to you as easily as your ideal life did. And the main reason for that is that the elements of your ideal path to wealth are not entirely of your choosing. You have your million-dollar goal. You know where you want to go. How you get there is laid out for you by a force and power that is not entirely or clearly understood by anyone except a Higher Authority.

You spend time daily on your million-dollar goal. You add to that goal that you are open and act upon the fastest, quickest, easiest way for you to manifest your first million dollars. You put a date, a year and a time stamp on it of your choosing. My personal recommendation is two to five years or sooner. It may be sooner, but it shouldn't be any longer. Five years should be long enough to pull together what you need to get to your million-dollar goal, especially in this day and age.

Now your job is to stay open and alert to the signs and signals that point your way to your million-dollar goal. You can't force it. You can't hurry it. You must be patient. It's a gift to you and for you from the other side. It is a gift that results from your focus on your goal, which focuses your thoughts which, in turn, set the wheels in motion for you.

Just go about your business, but be alert to the signs. These may come in the form of a sudden and powerful thought about something. It may come to you in the form of a person sharing an idea with you. It may come in the form of an ad you see. Whatever it is, it will sufficiently impress you that you will take notice and know that it was a sign that was meant for you. You'll know it. And your intuition will confirm it. And once you have that confirmation, go with it!

Do not question it, even if it doesn't make sense for you at the moment. Your path to your million-dollar goal will take several twists and turns along the way. There is a reason for everything that comes up for you. You may not see it right away. But each piece is part of the larger puzzle. And over time, you will see how each piece fits together perfectly, and how it could not have happened any other way.

You have another decision to make here: Whether you want to achieve your million-dollar goal over your 40-year working career as a professional or an employee, or accelerate the process by developing a business that allows you to accomplish the same goal in two to five years. Neither one is right or wrong. Neither one is good or bad. Only you can decide which way you want to go. Also, these methods are not mutually exclusive. Yours could be a hybrid, if you choose to go that way. Many people have a job, or a career, or a profession, and find ways to increase their income and make their financial plans outside of that avenue happen more quickly for them.

If you decide to go the route of a job, a career or a profession, then you must be especially mindful of the Money Rules outlined in Chapter Seven. These money rules apply to the wealthy and the not-so-wealthy alike. These are basic and time-tested rules for the management of your money. They have been around a long time. Whichever way you choose to go, you need to live your financial life by them. These rules will ensure that you will be able to manage your financial affairs over the long term, and that you will be financially prepared in your later years.

To recap these rules, you start by paying yourself, or saving at least 10% of everything you earn or receive over time. How long do you do this? Forever. When can you spend it? Never. It's not there to buy stuff. It's there as part of your long-term financial assets. Remember that saving $300 a month over 40 years, and earning 10% compound interest, can net you nearly $2 million. True, that rate of interest is hard to find today, but you get the idea.

Watch your expenses. Don't always run yourself down to your last dollar. Discipline yourself and learn to live below your means. Own your own place. Learn to invest in additional income-producing rental properties. Avoid consumer debt like the plague. Use credit cards sparingly and only when necessary. Make sure you pay them off as quickly as you can. This goes for student loans, as well. Pay them off as quickly as you can. Remember that the interest on your debt compounds a lot faster than the interest on your savings and investments, because banks and finance companies can charge you interest rates that would embarrass even a loan shark.

This is all part of protecting your money and managing it well. Resist the temptation of buying new and expensive stuff when you're just getting started. You'll be able to do that when you have the money in the bank, or when your investments are producing more income than your expenses. Be patient.

By following these rules, you will not only make your life a lot more financially manageable, you will be preparing yourself financially for your later years. Remember our statistic that 60% of people reach retirement age without any savings or investments to comfort and cushion them for the years that remain. They must rely on Social Security, which isn't much, and the generosity of family and friends. Getting old is not a choice. Unfortunately, it's something that happens to all of us. Best to keep it on your radar screen and prepare for it as best as you can. Learn and adopt these rules, and you will be financially ahead of more than 95% of the American public. I'm assuming here that your million-dollar goal is part of the plan.

And let's not forget the constant need to improve your Wealthability. <u>Your lifelong journey of wealth creation requires a lifelong interest in learning, especially learning about finances and investments. Read books. Take classes and courses. Attend lectures and seminars. Become friends with financially successful people that you want to emulate and with whom you want to associate. In short, put learning about wealth, finances and investments</u>

on your daily radar screen, and keep it there permanently.

And don't forget to budget for charitable giving. Your new motto is "Give and you shall receive." In actuality, you can only give to yourself. Whether it's your money or your time, giving warms the heart. It's also karma. What you put out comes back to you. Remember that giving not only helps other people, but it helps you develop your wealth mindset of prosperity and abundance. People who fear giving, because they fear not having enough for themselves, are coming from a mindset of scarcity, lack and poverty. This is negative thinking. And in your newfound wealth mindset, there is no room for negativity, lack or scarcity. So get rid of it. Be generous.

And now, if you choose to go down your fastest path possible for reaching your million-dollar goal, brace yourself for a wild ride. You'll be blazing a new trail that no one has ever been down before, at least not exactly the one you'll be going down. But before you start blazing, remember, the money rules stated above apply as much to you as they do to your more conservative friends. These rules provide the financial foundation on which you can build anything. Follow them. Incorporate them into your life as a matter of course. They will serve you well and provide a sense of satisfaction and encouragement as you move along your path to your million-dollar goal.

Alright, here we go. You are going to be a millionaire. You have made the decision that you will be a millionaire.. This is the path for you. And you have given yourself somewhere between two and five years to get there. You have your million-dollar goal written out, along with the statement that you are open and act upon the fastest, quickest and easiest way to create, attract and manifest your first million dollars. On the other side of your 3x5 card, you have your two declarations. The first is that "you will have your first million dollars by whatever date, year you choose, or sooner, without breaking a sweat." Your second declaration is that "you are worthy and deserve to have your first million dollars by the date of your choosing, or sooner, without breaking a sweat." YOU WILL REVIEW THIS CARD EVERY DAY, TWICE A DAY, WITH EMOTION, UNTIL THE DAY YOU FINALLY ACHIEVE YOUR MILLION-DOLLAR GOAL. PERIOD. NO EXCUSES. NO FAILING. UNDERSTAND? THIS IS NOW PART OF YOUR DAILY LIFE AND ROUTINE. IT IS WHAT WILL KEEP YOU ON TRACK TO YOUR GOAL. THIS IS VITALLY, CRITICALLY IMPORTANT!

By doing this, you are first and foremost reprogramming your mind into a new wealth mindset that allows you to believe that this can be done, that you are fully capable of getting this done, that you deserve to accomplish this, and that this will indeed come to pass. This won't happen overnight. But you will see and feel a dramatic change in your wealth outlook and core beliefs about wealth in about four to six weeks. It will just amaze you.

Now, by doing this simple exercise twice a day, you have learned that, by virtue of your new focus and these new thoughts, you are ordering your ever-faithful subconscious mind-servant to get to work, and bring these new things that you are now focusing on to you. Your wish is its command. And by so commanding, you have unleashed the power of the Law of Attraction, which by its very nature will attract to you the exact elements you need to achieve your million-dollar goal.

This is where it gets a little tricky. Your path is not laid out for you in 1-2-3 order. And it does not necessarily conform to your preconceived notion of what it should be, or is, or will be. The Universe is infinite, and by its very nature can see infinitely more possibilities and connections than you can with your five senses. Trust it. It is doing everything you want it to for your own benefit, well-being and satisfaction. It doesn't know what to do except that which you have asked it to do. Trust it and trust yourself.

This is both an exhilarating experience and a scary one. You have to trust something that you can't see. And you have to believe enough in yourself to trust yourself. This is where your intuition plays such a critical role. Get out of your head and stop trying to make sense of everything, and get in touch with your gut. You will be feeling your way through much of this process, not thinking your way through it. And in the process, you will have to learn to **get out of your own way**, trust yourself and your intuition, and follow the path that is being given to you, that is being shown to you, that is being laid out for you.

Welcome to the world of uncharted waters. Your intuition will be your guide. It will not only serve as a compass to point you in the right direction, your intuition will serve as your gyroscope, keeping you on track toward your million-dollar goal, regardless of what forces, events and circumstances arise to push you off your path. And your daily thoughts and declarations are what will enable your subconscious mind, the Law of Attraction, and your intuition to keep you on that track.

Now remember to watch for the signs. "Without breaking a sweat" means you don't worry about How you will get there. Don't be anxious about it. Don't worry about it. Just relax. The How is being shown to you as your path unfolds. Have faith. Believe in yourself. It will come to you in bits and pieces: a thought here, a feeling there, a person here, serendipity there. You don't know what it will be. Just stay focused on your million-dollar goal and expect the unexpected. That will be the norm.

When you receive these signs and signals, you will know that they are intended for you. You will feel it and your intuition will confirm it. Just stay alert and open. Once you receive and recognize them, you must then take the action they require: do something, meet someone. Your job is to follow through on whatever signs and signals are given to you. The accumulation of these little signs and signals and your follow-through are what will make your million-dollar goal a reality.

That's it. This is the process. You follow your path this way, and do the things you need to do, and you will inevitably be a millionaire. It cannot be otherwise. For these are the wheels you have set in motion. This is the process by which everyone else who has ever achieved great things has done so. The Laws are the same for you as they were for them. No different.

Before we close, let me add a couple of things you should keep in mind that I have found useful for myself.

Creating a business from scratch may be overwhelming for you. As it will unfold and develop piecemeal, I think you should take a deep breath and give yourself a chance and the wiggle room you need to at least get yourself started. Don't overthink it. Just allow yourself to grow into it. Like growing up day to day, you won't notice any real difference until you compare one year with the next. Give it your best shot for a year, and take a good look at yourself then. I think you will be amazed at what you see.

Successful businesses are generally the result of good business relationships. This is especially important when it comes to the people with whom you choose to surround yourself. If you're an idea person, then you need to partner with someone who is a born strategist, who can connect the dots and come up with a workable plan. You may be a natural analyst or the supportive type that loves the details of a project. Whatever business personality type you are, you should seek to associate with individuals who complement your natural strengths, gifts and talents. This doesn't mean you have to make them a partner. It just means you have to find people that can complement you, and bring something to the table that you don't have.

In some circles, a like-minded group like this that comes together to support a business idea is called a Mastermind Group or a Dream Team. I bring this up before we sign off because, as you develop your million-dollar idea, chances are that you will have to develop a group like this at some point. You may need expert advice with specific knowledge, business contacts and other connections. I thought you should be aware of it. Don't worry about this now. Just keep this in the back of your mind for use at a later date.

A year from now, you will begin to see the fruit of your labors. And with this will come an increased sense of self-confidence and daring. You won't be as intimidated as you were when you began this process. You'll have both increased confidence and courage to take even bolder steps in the direction of your million-dollar goal. You'll know that the path you're on is yours. In short, you'll get better at this game. You will have increased your business skills. You will have made new contacts. You will have found new advisers. And, as a result, you'll have more confidence and more faith in yourself.

In closing, let me remind you that the decision you made in the beginning to be a millionaire has changed and refocused your entire life. You are in the minority of individuals that take control of their lives by taking control of their thoughts. You have now set yourself on a path that will set you free financially, so you can be the person you were meant to be, live the life you were born to live, and make the unique contribution to the world that only you can make.

I'm so very proud of you. I hope someday to meet you and have an opportunity to listen to your amazing story.

Here's wishing you wealth, joy and happiness.

Rich Patenaude

Suggested Reading (one book at a time...)

<u>Wealth-building Classics</u>

The Richest Man in Babylon by George Clayson (1926)
Free on the internet as a PDF (http://www.ccsales.com/the_richest_man_in_ba bylon.pdf)

The Magic of Believing by Claude Bristol (1944)

Think and Grow Rich by Napoleon Hill (1937) (Remains the all-time bestseller on creating wealth)

<u>Millennial Generation Millionaires</u>

Reallionaire by Farrah Gray

Get Real, Get Rich by Farrah Gray

Nothing to Lose, Everything to Gain by Ryan Blair

Millionaire Mindset & Business Models

The One Minute Millionaire by Mark Victor Hansen & Robert G Allen

Cash in a Flash by Mark Victor Hansen & Robert G Allen

The Automatic Millionaire by David Bach

Secrets of the Millionaire Mind by T. Harv Eker

Rich Dad Poor Dad by Robert Kiyosaki and Sharon Lechter

The Millionaire Next Door by Thomas Stanley and William Danko

The Education of Millionaires by Michael Ellsberg

Real Estate & Finances

Nothing Down for the 2000's by Robert G Allen

Catch Fire by Douglas Scott Nelson

MONEY by Lee Jenkins

Personal Development

Psycho-Cybernetics 2000 by Maxwell Maltz

Outwitting the Devil by Napoleon Hill (Kept
hidden for 75 years as too controversial)

The Purpose-Driven Life by Rick Warren

Made in the USA
Coppell, TX
18 November 2020